LINDA
CLARK'S
COOKBOOK

LINDA CLARK'S COOKBOOK

Linda Clark

A Treasury of Recipes
for Successful Entertaining

Strawberry Hill Press

Strawberry Hill Press
616 44th Avenue
San Francisco, California 94121

Distributed by Stackpole Books
Cameron & Kelker Sts.
Harrisburg, Pa. 17105

First Printing, October, 1977

Manufactured in the United States of America

Illustrated by Ku, Fu-sheng

Book design by Carlton Clark Herrick

Library of Congress Cataloging in Publication Date

Clark, Linda A.
   Linda Clark's Cookbook.

   Includes index.
   1. Cookery.   2. Menus.   I. Title.
TX715.C5776   1977   641.5   77-8716
ISBN 0-89407-009-6

Other Books by Linda Clark

Available at Health Stores or May be Ordered Through Bookstores.
Most are in Paperback.

Stay Young Longer
Get Well Naturally
Secrets of Health and Beauty
Help Yourself to Health (an ESP Book)
Know Your Nutrition
Be Slim and Healthy
Face Improvement
Through Exercise and Nutrition
Are You Radioactive?
How to Protect Yourself
Rejuvenation
Color Therapy
Health, Youth and Beauty Through Color Breathing
(with Yvonne Martine)
Beauty Questions and Answers (with Karen Kelly)
Handbook of Natural Remedies For Common Ailments
Health and Beauty For Your Pets
Through Nutrition
The Best of Linda Clark
An Anthology

Note: Due to a crowded schedule, Linda Clark
        cannot correspond with readers.

Dedicated to my two daughters
Joan and Karen
Who have always been fans of my cooking
and whose children (a total of seven)
are beginning to follow suit

Table of Contents

Author's Warning

Before you read this cookbook, as a reporter in nutrition and health, I must warn you that the recipes which follow are not necessarily health recipes. At heart, I am a gourmet cook and loathe humdrum food. I definitely feel that even health foods can be gourmet eating, and the two can often be combined by substituting healthful ingredients for non-healthful ones. Traditionally, many recipes are often considered sacred and people think they should not be changed, even though they originally called for loads of white sugar, or white flour, or whatever our ancestors used.

Times have changed. We now know that too much sugar is not good for us, and flours other than white flour are more nutritious. So healthful ingredients *can* and should be substituted in many recipes, but not all. Does this mean we should avoid such wonderful traditional or delicious recipes entirely? Perish the thought! Eating should preferably be healthful. But I feel strongly that eating should also be fun. Psychologically, it should still be one of our few pleasures left today when other pleasures are disappearing down the drain (energy crises, money shortages, etc.). So I do not object to going berserk occasionally and eating something which is good, though not necessarily good for you. Neither should you. It is what you eat every day which builds your body toward health. An occasional lapse is not going to do you in.

3

The recipes which follow are delicious ones which have rated loud applause from the majority. But because substitutions were not always possible for a successful result, I have mostly left them in their traditional form. Therefore I warn you: *they are not necessarily health recipes* and I am making no bones about it! They make for good eating and psychological pleasure, which is surely worth something in today's world. These recipes are also not original but have been borrowed over a lifetime because they are so delicious.

They are not grouped together under soups, salads, entrées, etc., but are arranged in menus. Knowing that hosts or hostesses are wondering what in the world to serve guests, I am sure they need help with the entire menu. If you wish to make changes, ad lib if you prefer. The individual recipes can be found in the index. If exact measurements or cooking times are not mentioned, don't panic. *A good cook should be a creative cook.* Most good cooks *are* creative, and pay little attention to many exact measurements, preferring a pinch of this, a dash of that, tasting as they go. So if you do not find exact amounts, start tasting and adding such things as herbs, salt, etc. — but *slowly*. You can always add more, but you can't take too much out. (After this effort, if anyone automatically salts my food before tasting it, he will get dark looks from me.)

Tips for success:

4

Adjust your type of entertaining to your needs and wishes. I serve food buffet-style almost entirely because it is easier for me and usually for the guests. And don't expect everyone to like the same things. As I said, these recipes brought raves from the majority. This is enough for me. And I don't know about you, but I cannot cook with any-one else in the kitchen talking to me. I may add too much salt or let something burn. If you feel the same way, say so! Shoo the intruder into the other room, explaining your in-adequacies. It may spell the difference between success and failure in one dish or an entire meal.

Because this book includes recipes for pure enjoyment, instead of exclusively for health, I wanted to call it *Let's Cook it Wrong* with apologies to Adelle Davis, who wrote *Let's Cook it Right,* a truly nutritional, healthful cookbook. But the publisher wouldn't let me. He is probably right. Even so, I am going to let you into a secret about Adelle. Years ago, I and a group of others, were weekending at her house. Naturally we expected to be fortified with nutritional meals, and mostly we were. But on opening night we were unprepared for a pleasant shock.

Adelle was her own cook and the beginning of that first meal came up to all health expectations. Then, at dessert time, with a wicked gleam in her eye she asked to be excused and said she would not be back for awhile, but to sit tight. When she returned, she was carrying aloft a Baked Alaska, dripping with sugar, chocolate, ice cream and every no-no in her book. (Baked Alaska is about as far from a health food as you can get.) But we all fell to and wolfed it down with relish.

I am not going to give you a recipe for Baked Alaska. You can find it in almost any traditional cookbook. But neither am I going to apologize for the recipes which follow, even if they do contain nutritional no-nos.

Since, as I said before, it is what you eat *regularly* which is good for you, a lapse now and then is not going to do you in. So the recipes which follow may be considered lapses. But enjoy them anyway. Above all, *don't feel guilty.* If Adelle, who introduced us to good nutrition, could enjoy them, so can we.

Linda Clark

5

P.S. Any brand names I have used are not paid commercials. The manufacturers will learn about them for the first time on these pages. Also, if I find better ones in the future, I will use them, instead.

Menu I

A Favorite Dinner
Baked Fried Chicken
Spoon Corn Bread
Green Salad
Ambrosia

Baked Fried Chicken:

Chicken fryer(s) cut up
Melted Butter or margarine
Pepperidge Farm herb-flavored stuffing
Sea Salt (Chico San brand from health stores)

Dip each piece of chicken first in melted butter or margarine, then in the Pepperidge Farm herb-flavored **7** stuffing bread crumbs. (If crumbs are too large to stick to the chicken, crush with a rolling pin or whiz quickly only the larger crumb pieces in the blender.)

Arrange pieces on a broiling pan with a perforated tray so that melted butter can run off. Add a shake or so of sea salt on each chicken piece and bake until crisp and crunchy and light brown, approximately for one hour at 350°. (The crumbs which fall off are even better than the chicken.) I urge guests to eat this chicken with their fingers and supply plenty of paper napkins.

This recipe has a history. It has been a favorite in our family for many years. I was originally introduced to it by a friend who made it and served it cold (we prefer it hot) for a lunch she took in her station wagon to a Harvard-Yale football game. When I asked for the recipe I found that she used crushed corn flakes (dry cereal) as the coating. I do not believe in corn flakes which are so refined that nutritionists have learned they contain little more nutrition than the pasteboard box in which they are sold. Besides, they are relatively tasteless.

So I hunted for and found a better substitute which was delicious: a cereal called corn soya flakes. Unfortunately, since this dry cereal contained no sugar, children would not eat it. Therefore it was discontinued by the manufacturer. I continued to hunt and finally found the *Pepperidge Farm herb-flavored stuffing* bread crumbs which are perfect. I find *no other* substitute works as well!

There is no standing over the stove required to prepare this "fried" chicken. Nor is it greasy like regular fried chicken, if cooked as directed. Put it in the oven and forget it. Easy!

Spoon Corn Bread

>3 cups milk
>3 eggs
>1 scant cup of yellow cornmeal (undegerminated from
>   health store)
>1 tablespoon butter
>3 teaspoons baking powder
>1 teaspoon salt

Stir meal into 2 cups of milk, and let come to a boil stirring constantly to avoid lumps. When it reaches the mushy stage, add balance of milk, well-beaten eggs, salt, baking powder and melted butter. Mix well. Bake in a greased earthenware or pyrex flat casserole or in an iron skillet. Bake at 325°, 45 to 60 minutes or until firm through the middle and lightly brown on top. Serve in the pan in which it was cooked. Cut in pie-shaped wedges, top each piece with a pat of butter and eat with a fork or spoon.

Green Salad

I am fussy about my salads but nothing could be easier. This is a version of a French salad introduced to me by Adelle Davis. Break up several types of lettuce into bite size and place in a large salad bowl. Add any other raw garden vegetables in season: fresh peas, cucumber slices, green pepper slices, sliced raw Jerusalem artichoke (tastes like water chestnuts and is delicious), red onion rings for color and flavor, and anything else which is crunchy and good.

Serve cold! *Just* before serving, add enough oil (olive or an oil blend from health store) to barely coat the vegetables without wilting them, and toss. Then add some fresh lemon juice or garlic wine vinegar to flavor (taste as you go). Add sea salt, and, if you like it, some fresh ground black pepper. I often add a handful of Pepperidge Farm croutons at this point. There are other croutons on the market but these have the fewest additives. They come in several flavors. I prefer the onion-garlic.

Ambrosia

This dessert should be made the day before and refrigerated. It takes a bit of doing, but is worth it, since there is no last minute panic in preparing it. It is a Southern standby, with different versions. Here is mine:

Peel and cut up 6 to 8 large oranges into bite size. Save any juice possible, adding it to the orange which should be placed in a large bowl. Add the contents of one package of tiny marshmallows. Add approximately ¼ cup of shredded coconut, fresh or canned, preferably without sugar. Then add approximately ½ cup of blanched almond bits (not slices), available in small packets at grocery stores. Add unsweetened pineapple juice to cover all, stir lightly and refrigerate. The marshmallows become very soft as they absorb the juice. Add more juice later if too dry. Serve in stemmed glassware for drama.

9

Menu II

Breakfast, Brunch or Lunch No. 1

Juice or Fruit in Season
Nero Wolfe's Scrambled Eggs;
or Omelet;
or Baked Eggs
Blueberry Bran Muffins

This menu is flexible and can be served any time in the forenoon or at noon, particulary if unexpected guests arrive for lunch and you have nothing else on hand. The omelet does not take long; the baked eggs or Nero Wolfe's scrambled eggs only a little longer. The muffins can be made first, and while they are baking you can put the baked eggs in the oven at the same time, or a few minutes later. Or start the scrambled eggs on top of the stove — they take approximately the same time as the muffins. You can always turn off the oven and let the muffins keep warm and serve them later with coffee if you wish. Don't panic. Your guests can enjoy the fruit or juice while you prepare the rest of the food. Keep it easy so the guests will feel easy, too. Everyone will be happier if you are relaxed. A few minutes here or there aren't all that important.

Rex Stout, in his "whodunnits," featuring that gourmet detective, Nero Wolfe, and his luscious foods, has included this recipe for delectable scrambled eggs in his book, *Nero Wolfe's Cookbook* (Viking Press, 1973).

Nero Wolfe's scrambled Eggs

6 large eggs
1 cup light cream
½ teaspoon salt
2 tablespoons butter

Heat water in lower part of a double boiler and bring to a boil. Reduce to a simmer and keep it at a simmer (no boiling throughout the entire cooking). Beat eggs, cream and seasoning. Drop the butter in the top part of the double boiler and let it melt, while you are beating the eggs, cream and salt in the blender, or with a wire whisk in a bowl.

Pour this mixture on top of the melted butter in the top of the double boiler. Cover and let cook undisturbed for 15 minutes. Remove the lid and stir continuously with a wooden spoon, until the desired state of done-ness. (Scrambled eggs should not be too dry.)

12 Remove from pan. (Nero Wolfe serves his scrambled eggs with a dash of paprika on top.) In the cookbook there is an additional sauce to cover the eggs, which I consider too complicated. However, you can change the flavor of the eggs from time to time (after a home dress rehearsal) by adding dried onion flakes, chopped parsley or chives, or a shake (and I do mean a shake only) of "fines herbes" seasoning. I use Spice Islands brand. I think you and your guests will be impressed with the wonderful texture of these scrambled eggs. If you make less than the recipe, cook for a shorter time.

Omelets

Omelets can be dramatic, interesting and change-able, depending upon what you find in the refrigerator. All you do is dream up a new filling.

If you want a Spanish omelet, lightly sauté some fresh tomatoes, onion, green pepper, and set aside to keep warm in one pan until you are ready to add it to the omelet you have made in another. Grated cheese makes a good filling. (I grate my cheese in a blender.) Another possibility: have some left over mushrooms? Slice and sauté in butter. Or, any ends of ham? Dice, maybe add green pepper and onion, sauté all, and you've got another filling. You can become expert with omelets if you use your ingenuity.

The main problem with omelets is that you can make only one at a time. But guests do not seem to mind waiting. Encourage each one to eat his the minute you serve it without waiting for the others.

Omelets are easy to make, but in case you might get stage fright at your first public try, get the "feel" by experimenting ahead of time on yourself or your family until it becomes second nature.

Omelet Recipe

1 or 2 eggs per person. Put in blender, with one table-spoon cream, milk, or half-and-half for *each* egg. Add a shake of sea salt. Blend at high speed for several minutes until eggs are frothy and contain plenty of air. While this is happening, drop butter into your pan, preferably a small frying pan with rounded sides, and heat on a *low* heated burner. If the butter burns, throw it out and start over. Burned butter will ruin any good omelet.

Pour the briskly beaten eggs into the warm, buttered pan, still on low heat. When the eggs on the bottom have solidified, use your pancake turner to pull them away from the edges of the pan and tip slightly to let the uncooked eggs run off to the sides so that they, too, can become firm.

While the middle is still soft, spread over the top whatever filling you have already prepared and have set aside to keep warm. Wait a minute, then flip over half of the omelet sideways in the pan to cover the other half, like a half moon. Wait a few minutes more for interior cooking. You may have to flip over the whole thing onto its other side to completely cook the inside egg mixture, but it won't take but a minute or so to finish. Serve with a flourish; perhaps topped with some chopped parsley or chives or whatever variation you have already tried out at a home dress rehearsal with successful results.

Once you get the knack, and it isn't hard to do, you can become famous for your omelets.

Baked Eggs

In case you do not want to be a short order cook and cook the previously described scrambled eggs or omelet, you can substitute baked eggs which require no watching. Unfortunately, I cannot give you exact ¹irections for variations since this is a creative dish. Plain baked eggs are fixed as follows: put a lump of butter or margarine in the bottom of a custard cup. Break in a whole egg. Cover with half-and-half, a shake or so of dried onion flakes, salt, and top with Pepperidge Farm herb-flavored stuffing crumbs. Bake at 325° for approximately 20 minutes, or until the egg mixture has "set." The yolk will be firm.

14

For variations, substitute grated cheese for onion flakes and crumbs. Or top with a slice of tomato, or with sliced mushrooms. Experiment. You may come up with some exciting innovations. You may wish to take orders from your guests. Nothing is more disconcerting than providing mushrooms for everyone, only to find that some people don't like mushrooms. Even last-minute orders can be accommodated for baked eggs, since cooking time is short. Bake at 325° until firm, or at muffin temperature for less time.

Now for those muffins which are always a success!

Even if everything else flops, no one will remember once they have tried a muffin. The beautiful part about these muffins is that they are considered good for you! Doctors and other health specialists have rediscovered bran which, taken regularly, keeps your innards in clockwork condition and can even prevent intestinal disorders, they say. Your guests will bless you for this method of using bran rather than trying to gulp it down dry, or on cereal.

Blueberry Bran Muffins

Dry Ingredients

In a bowl combine:

1 cup unbleached flour
1 cup bran flakes (from health store — I use no other kind)
3 teaspoons baking powder
1 cup fresh or dry frozen unsweetened blueberries, or raisins, or chopped apples, or reconstituted dried apricots, or other choices (better experiment ahead of time)

Wet Ingredients

In blender, mix:

1 egg
1 cup milk
Honey to taste — about 3 tablespoons
3 tablespoons of oil

Blend the wet ingredients. Add to the dry ingredients and stir, *don't beat.* If the batter is not stiff, but runny, add a bit more bran. Spoon into half-filled, oiled muffin pans and bake at 400° until brown — about 30 minutes, but watch them! If you are lucky enough to have any left, split and toast another day for your own breakfast. In any case, serve with butter.

Menu III

Breakfast, Brunch or Lunch No. 2
Fruit or Juice in Season
Quiche
Streusel — Filled Coffee Cake

Quiche was formerly known as Quiche Lorraine, since it originated in that area of France. Now the name Lorraine is being dropped, new variations are being introduced, and the dish, a delicious one, is merely called Quiche.

The original Quiche was always made in a prebaked pie shell. This is O.K., but not necessary. Buttered Pepperidge Farm herb-flavored stuffing crumbs can be used, mixed with butter, as a crumb crust, or you really need no crust at all. Less calories this way.

Quiche also originally had crumbled cooked bacon sprinkled over the bottom of the pie shell. I love bacon but refuse to eat it as long as it contains those dangerous additives, nitrates and nitrites. I will not elaborate here, but if you want to take the chance, go ahead; I personally will skip it. Quiche often contains a mild tasting Swiss, Gruyere or Monterey Jack cheese, although the original version did not contain cheese, at least according to Julia Child. But if you want it, grate one cup of cheese and sprinkle it over the crust or bottom of the pie plate, pyrex preferred. Here is a good version of the filling:

Quiche

3 large eggs
¼ teaspoon *each* salt and nutmeg. Pinch of pepper.
½ cup heavy cream
1½ tablespoons butter

Beat the mixture in a blender or by hand and pour into pie shell or plain pie plate, with or without bacon or cheese underneath. Sautéed onions or dried onion flakes may be added to the mixture, if you wish.

Pour mixture into pan, no higher than ½ inch from the top rim or it will run over into your oven. *It is better to have too little than too much.* Cut butter into small pieces and arrange on top. Place pan in a preheated 375° oven. Cook for 30 to 35 minutes, until slightly brown on top, or firm in the middle when tested by a skewer. Remove from oven and cut into pie-shaped wedges, as you serve it.

The best Quiche I have ever eaten had Swiss cheese, a bit of onion, and a generous amount of chopped cooked spinach in it. I don't have the recipe, unfortunately, but you can improvise. Mushrooms are another possibility. Use your own ingenuity for creating still other innovations. Creative cookery is fun!

Streusel-Filled Coffee Cake

18

One of my daughters supplied this recipe. Be prepared for guests to ask for seconds.

1½ cups unbleached flour
3 tablespoons baking powder
¼ cup shortening (oil or margarine, or butter if you
   can afford it)
¼ cup milk
½ teaspoon sea salt
¾ cup raw sugar
1 egg
1 teaspoon vanilla

To dry ingredients, cut in solid shortening or mix oil with milk and beaten egg plus vanilla. Add liquids to dry ingredients. Mix well, but do not beat. Pour half of the batter into a greased 6" x 10" pan. Sprinkle with the streusel filling, add rest of batter and sprinkle with remaining streusel. Bake for thirty minutes in a 350° oven.

Streusel Filling

(Note from my daughter: "I often double this part of the recipe.")

½ cup chopped nuts
½ cup brown sugar
2 tablespoons flour
2 teaspoons cinnamon
2 tablespoons melted butter

Mix all ingredients.

Menu IV

Make Ahead Dinner

Beef Marinade
Brown Rice
Green Salad with Special Dressing
Carrot Cake

This recipe for Beef Marinade is super. Adults and children of all ages go for it. My friend Anne D. got it second hand from Canada and you can cook it all at once or save half of it for the following day. It keeps well, uncooked, if refrigerated.

Marinade
¾ cup oil
½ cup soy sauce
¼ cup mild honey
2 tablespoons apple cider vinegar
½ onion, chopped
2 garlic cloves, minced
1½ teaspoons ginger
Get a flank steak (two lbs. can be served for two separate days)

Marinate the steak in the mixed ingredients above, all placed in a 13" x 9" pyrex dish. Keep in the refrigerator for two days, turning the meat twice daily. When ready to cook, broil the flank steak for 5 minutes on each side, and cut into diagonal slices. The meat juice is good when served with the brown rice.

Special French Dressing

This French dressing recipe was given to me by a chef before he departed from a well-known restaurant famous in my area. You may wish to make it up and have it ready to pour over your green salad of lettuce and vegetables which have been washed, dried, chilled and kept crisp in a plastic bag in the refrigerator. Do not drown the salad; merely lightly coat the leaves of lettuce and other vegetables with it. It is excellent.

For one pint:

Mix:
Wine vinegar (2/5)
Olive oil (3/5)
Dry mustard (to taste)
1 scant teaspoon raw sugar
salt, pepper, and a dash of Spice Islands *Salad Herbs* mixture (no other herb mixture)
3 crushed garlic cloves or garlic salt

If this recipe sounds mysterious, it is because the chef reduced it from a recipe for making a gallon of the dressing for the restaurant to a smaller amount most of us would use at home. The fractions of oil and vinegar refer to the ratio of oil to vinegar, no matter how much or how little you make.

Carrot Cake

(Contributed by one of my health-minded daughters)

Mix:

- 2 cups unbleached flour
- 2 cups raw sugar or 2/3 cup honey
- 2 teaspoons salt
- 2 teaspoons baking powder
- 2 teaspoons cinnamon
- Add 1½ cups oil (Stir well)
- Add 4 large eggs, one at a time, mixing well after each addition.
- Add 3 cups of grated raw carrots (or they can be put through a meat grinder)
- 1 cup nuts

Bake at 350° for one hour, in a tube pan; or in two cake layer pans for 30 to 45 minutes.

This cake is best the second day. It really needs no icing but if you insist, here is a recipe:

Creme ½ stick butter or margarine with 2 ozs. cream cheese, 2 teaspoons vanilla, ½ box powdered sugar and enough milk to make the right consistency for spreading.

Menu V

Unusual Dinner
BBQ Spare Ribs
Baked Cheese Fondue
Green Salad
Mystery Fruit Cup

BBQ Spare Ribs

There must be about 100 versions of barbecued spare ribs and I have tried most of them. This recipe is my version of one provided by Ruth Mills Teague in a book, *Cooking for Company*, published as early as 1945. I have never found one to equal it, as all who rave over this recipe agree. I don't bother to cook it on an outdoor grill because it is easier to do indoors.

Get a strip of pork spare ribs, with as much meat and as little fat as possible. Lay it flat in a roasting pan and add a small amount of water. Cover and steam or simmer on top of the stove for several hours until fork tender. (If liquid boils dry, add more.) Let cool, separate individually each bone with its meat from the strip with a sharp-pointed knife.

While the ribs are cooking, make the following sauce, the secret of the success of this recipe.

Sauce

    5 tablespoons light brown sugar
    1/3 cup of soy sauce
    1 minced clove of garlic
    3 tablespoons candied ginger (I toss it in my blender to
        chop into small pieces)

Simmer slowly until syrupy, remove from heat and let stand until needed. Shortly before serving time, dip each spare rib in this sauce, placing all on a broiler pan and broil at a midway level in your oven until bubbly and browned. Turn the ribs over, spoon remaining sauce on the uncooked side and broil as before. Turn off your oven or set at "warm" and the ribs will stay warm while you assemble the rest of the menu. Serve ribs in a big bowl, platter, or paper-lined basket with plenty of paper napkins and a bone disposal dish. Obviously these delicious ribs are best eaten with the fingers. When buying the ribs, allow at least 5 to 6 per person. Any leftovers can be eaten cold or reheated the next day.

Baked Cheese Fondue

This recipe is another winner, borrowed from Virginia Stanton's book, *The House Beautiful Guide to Successful Entertaining*. Virginia, a neighbor of mine, is known internationally for her fabulous cooking. She was formerly party editor of *House Beautiful* magazine. She calls this recipe "Cheese Fondue Janie" and says it is the best luncheon or Sunday night supper dish she has ever found. Since most people think of cheese fondue as the drippy kind in which you plunge individual pieces of bread into a chafing dish sauce, I call this a *baked* fondue, which it is. I would suggest cooking it first, removing it from the oven while you broil the spare-ribs, then return it to the oven to keep warm with the spare ribs until you are ready to serve. It is not temperamental, like most cheese-egg dishes, and won't fall if set away to keep warm for about 20 minutes — the approximate time you need to broil the ribs. Here is my version of this famous dish:

Baked Cheese Fondue

    8 slices of slightly stale unbleached white bread, minus
        crusts
    6 eggs
    1½ to 2 pounds sharp cheddar cheese
    2½ cups of whole milk or half-and-half
    1 teaspoon (rounded) brown sugar
    1 chopped green onion (scallion) and stems (leaves)
    ½ teaspoon dry mustard
    ½ teaspoon Beau Monde (Spice Islands) seasoning
    ½ teaspoon Worcestershire sauce
    ½ teaspoon salt

Cut the crustless bread slices in small squares, about ½ inch or less. Grease the bottom of a casserole in which you will serve it. Put all liquids, seasonings and eggs into the blender. Cut cheese into medium-sized pieces and add to the liquids. Blend all until the cheese is about the size of particles if grated.

To assemble, put one layer of bread cubes on the bottom of the buttered casserole. Cover with the blended liquids. Repeat bread, then liquids, layer by layer, until all ingredients are used.

Cover the casserole with a lid or foil and store in the refrigerator over night. Remove next day, two hours before ready to cook, and let stand at room temperature.

Place the casserole in a 300° oven and bake one hour or until lightly brown. Serves 8.

27

Green Salad

    See Menu I

Mystery Fruit Cup

For dessert, your palate will need something fresh, crisp, and slightly sharp to contrast with the rest of the menu. Make a fruit cup of fruits in season, including some citrus. Make it ahead of time, and add a *pinch* of anise seed (the secret or mystery ingredient). Frankly I don't like anise seed, but adding a pinch to this and mixing with the fruit before refrigerating gives a haunting, unidentified flavor which causes everyone to ask what it is as they taste it. Coffee is a good follower of this meal.

Menu VI

Fancy Dinner
Mrs. M's Marvelous Stuffed Chicken
Fresh Corn Cakes
Green Vegetable in Season, steamed or stir-fried
Green Salad
Yogurt Pie

Mrs. M's Marvelous Stuffed Chicken

I have no idea who Mrs. M is since I cut this recipe from a magazine many years ago. And it *is* marvelous as well as unique. A do-ahead dish which keeps while your guests talk, are late, or drink cocktails. Choose ½ small young broiler or ½ Cornish hen for each guest.

½ cup heavy (whipped) cream
2 tablespoons butter
½ cup dry white wine
½ lb. fresh mushrooms
½ cup blanched almonds

Take ¼ cup of the heavy cream (you will need the rest later) and roll the chicken halves in the cream, again and again, getting it thoroughly into the outsides and cavities.

Sprinkle with salt and fresh black pepper, if you like it. Put the wine in the bottom of one or two casseroles (as needed). Place chickens cavity side down, and bake in a 325° oven for about an hour, basting tops occasionally with wine from bottom of the casserole.

Meanwhile, chop the mushrooms and toss into the 2 tablespoons of melted butter. Sauté lightly. After a minute or two add the rest of the cream. Now for the clincher: either pulverize the almonds in a blender, or in a rotary hand grinder grind them directly into the simmering mushrooms. The almond meal becomes the thickening. In a minute or two, it will puff up like fluffy whipped potatoes. Check for seasoning.

Remove the cooked chicken halves from the oven. Turn the chickens cavity side up and drop spoonfuls of the mushroom-almond mixture into each cavity. Sprinkle with fresh tarragon, or parsley and paprika. Turn oven very low (250°). Let rest in the oven until ready to serve; it improves on standing.

Fresh Corn Cakes

These corn cakes are the most! I can't take credit for the recipe which came off the wrapper of a little gadget which is called a corn scraper. The recipe is simple, but don't tamper with it, thinking you will make it better. No flour, no more eggs, no nothing! You can serve them for breakfast but I serve them as a savory vegetable topped only with a pat of butter. They will disappear in seconds.

Cut off the kernels of six ears of fresh corn. Put in the blender, add 1 egg and a shake of salt. Whiz until the mixture is almost smooth. Pour onto a hot griddle or electric skillet, a little at a time, like small pancakes, turning, when brown, with a pancake turner. Since I usually serve buffet-style I ask a willing helper to monitor the corn cakes. If people want refills, have the pitcher of batter ready beside the electric skillet and let them cook. (You needn't be a slave.) If it is not fresh corn season when you prepare this meal, substitute the potato pancakes in Menu XV.

Green Vegetable

Choose any green vegetable in season. Stir-fry in a bit of oil, Oriental style, till crisp and bright green, or steam in a steam-marvel. Never overcook your vegetables.

Green Salad

(see Menu I)

Yogurt Pie

This yogurt pie became famous at Farmer's Market in Los Angeles, and afterward sold out fast daily in a lunch-room of a prestigious store on Fifth Avenue in New York City. Make it the day before and be prepared with the recipe to give it to those who ask for it.

    1 graham cracker pie crust; buy or mix your own
    1 8 oz. package of Philadelphia cream cheese
    1 8 oz. container of smooth, creamed cottage cheese
      or use a second package of Philadelphia cream
      cheese, if you prefer.
    5 teaspoons mild flavored honey such as clover
    1 8 oz. container of plain yogurt
    1 envelope of plain, unflavored gelatin
    1 teaspoon vanilla

33

Soak the gelatine in ¼ cup of cold water to soften. Place cup (pyrex) over boiling water in a small pan until mixture has dissolved and liquified. Stir honey into gelatine. Cut up Philadelphia cream cheese and spoon together with cottage cheese and yogurt into the blender. Add gelatine-honey mixture, then vanilla, blending all until smooth. Pour over graham crust-lined pie plate.

Refrigerate over night. It can be garnished with fresh berries, or toasted almond slices, but is not necessary. Traditionally it is served plain.

Menu VII

Ladies Luncheon No. 1

Seafood Shells
Stuffed Avocado Salad
Crisp Bread Sticks
Canteloupe-Watermelon Balls with Mint
Hot Tea, or Minted Iced Tea

Seafood Shells

These shells are decorative, delicious and easy. I keep ingredients on hand at all times since they are perfect for the sudden unexpected appearance of a lunch guest, and can thus provide emergency flair and fare for a long-remembered, but prepared within minutes, lunch. I have never served these shells without a request for the recipe. So here it is:

35

1 can tuna fish
1 can mushroom soup (undiluted)
1 can drained, green asparagus spears and cuts

Mix the three ingredients, perhaps adding a dash of dried onion flakes. Spoon into shells. Top with Pepperidge Farm herb-flavored stuffing bread crumbs. Heat at 325° until bubbly (about 25 minutes).

The seashells, suitable for individual servings, are available at kitchen supply shops or kitchen supply departments in larger stores. You could substitute custard cups or other small heat-proof attractive containers.

Stuffed Avocado Salad

Either buy some canned tomato aspic or make your own as follows: buy a large can of tomato juice, soak 2 tablespoons of gelatine in ½ cup cold tomato juice. Heat 3½ cups of the remaining juice from the can, and taste for seaoning. You may wish to fortify it. (A few drops of lemon, perhaps a sprinkle of sugar, two drops of Worcestershire sauce, and possibly one shake of herbs, either basil or mixed — take it easy here — will make it tastier.) Dissolve gelatine over hot water and add mixture to hot, flavored, tomato juice. Stir well. Refrigerate the entire mixture in a bowl until nearly set.

Whether the aspic is bought or made, cut up raw crunchy vegetables into tiny cubes: cucumbers, celery, onion, green pepper, etc. and mix into the soft aspic. Return to refrigerator to become firm. When ready to serve, peel the avocado, cut in half, remove seed. Allow one half avocado for each person. Spoon the tomato aspic-vegetable mixture into the avocado cavity and top with a dollop of mayonnaise plus a dash of paprika. Serve on a leaf of lettuce on individual salad plates.

Bread sticks are available in most grocery stores, and usually from Italian bakers. Heat and cool them ahead of serving time so they will be crisp. Serve in a glass or upright vase, set on the table for self-help.

The crisp fresh fruit is a refreshing taste complement for this luncheon. Use canteloupe and melon balls or substitute fruit of your choice, including honeydew, seedless green grapes, fresh pineapple, or whatever is in season. Top with a mint leaf. Serve in stemmed champagne glasses or chubby cocktail glasses.

If the day is hot, do try the minted iced tea. I serve it by the gallon during hot weather and *without sugar,* although I have sugar ready for those who insist on it.

To make: Get *fresh* mint leaves (I grow my own in pots); mint tea bags will not suffice. The mint flavor must be fresh or skip the whole thing. Put a handful of mint leaves in a pyrex tea pot (4 to 6 cups), add one regular black-orange pekoe tea bag *per person* with an extra for the pot. Pour boiling water over all and let steep. Remove the tea bags as soon as the tea is the right color — perhaps 5 minutes. Leave the mint leaves to steep for extra flavor until serving time. Pour over ice cubes which have been placed in glasses. I often pour the hot tea directly over the cubes in each glass. If you need more tea, for a large group, make in advance and empty the tea as you make it from the tea pot into a large glass pitcher which holds more than the tea-pot. Don't stretch the mint leaves too far. Add more for a delightful refreshing flavor as needed.

Menu VIII

Italian Dinner

Lasagna
Italian Garlic Bread
Green Salad
Chianti or Dry Red Wine
Fresh Fruit or Fruit Cup

This recipe for lasagna is another family treasure which elicits oh's and ah's from guests. The recipe will serve six people generously and if your largest flat casserole isn't large enough, make two smaller ones. The meat sauce part of the recipe is also excellent for spaghetti, the best I have found. I owe this recipe's success to Midge R. who provided it.

Meat Sauce

Brown 2 onions, chopped, in olive oil until golden (not too dark). Add salt and pepper. Add two pounds of ground beef and sear meat lightly. Then add:

3 cans of tomato paste (small size)
3 cans of tomato sauce (medium to large size)
3 cans of water (medium size) (same as cans above)

When this boils, add 7 tablespoons olive oil, 1 bay leaf, 1 teaspoon oregano and 1 chopped clove of garlic. Let simmer, covered, for 2½ hours.

Lasagna

To finish this dish you will need 1 lb. of ricotta cheese, several packages of grated mozzarella cheese, a container of Parmesan cheese, and a package of wide lasagna noodles.

Cook the noodles until *under* tender, known to Italians as *al dente.*

Grease your largest casserole or two smaller ones with olive oil.

Line the casserole with the cooked noodles.

Top with a layer of ricotta cheese, then a layer of meat sauce, followed by a layer of Parmesan cheese, more meat sauce, then a layer of mozzarella cheese, noodles, repeating all layers and finally topping with Parmesan cheese.

Bake in a 325° oven about ¾ of an hour or until bubbly.

Italian Garlic Bread

Italian garlic bread is rarely served to the American public. I was invited to watch its preparation in the kitchen of a true Italian restaurant. Here is the method:

In the morning of the day to serve the bread, cut up lots of garlic into small pieces. Add to Italian olive oil in a pyrex dish. Let stand all day. (I prefer to add salt.)

At serving time, slice a long loaf of French bread *lengthwise,* into two long slabs. Place on a cookie sheet, cut sides up. Pour oil with minced garlic chips over each slab, then place under a broiler, toasting the bread and the garlic chips simultaneously. On removing from oven, quickly cut slabs into wide chunks, about 3 to 4 inches in width. Pile into a basket, cover with a napkin to keep hot until it reaches the table. If you have not eaten this type of garlic bread, you have a new experience awaiting you.

Obviously a crisp green salad dressed only with oil and vinegar, salt and fresh ground pepper, is called for. And dry, red wine is traditionally served with this Italian meal.

No dessert, except fresh fruit, is needed.

Menu IX

Ladies' Luncheon No. 2
(Men are welcome)

Venetian Liver
Raw Vegetable Plate
Tea, hot or iced; Coffee, hot or iced
Fabulous Nut Cake

Venetian Liver

This recipe is another with a history. It was served by a faculty wife to other faculty wives of a well-known Eastern University. The hostess' mother was living in Venice and had provided the recipe. It is an unusual dish, one of those which is free-lance, not made with exact measurement but with "pinches of this" and "dashes of that." Even so, and in spite of the fact that many people believe they do not like liver, *every* guest left this particular luncheon with the requested recipe tucked in her purse. So don't sell it short until you have tried it in dress rehearsal.

Cut into cubes approximately ¼ pound of calves' or baby beef liver. If the liver has been frozen, so much the better. It is easier to cut while frozen, but let it thaw before cooking.

In a frying pan, put a few tablespoons of mixed butter and olive oil. Sauté lightly some chopped onion, but not until brown. Then turn up the heat for browning and drop in the liver cubes, tossing until browned on the outside and just past the rare stage on the inside. Add a shake or so of salt, and several pinches of *powdered* sage leaves (perhaps one pinch per person). Toss again. Now pour medium dry Vermouth over all, but not quite enough to cover. Turn the heat low and stir. Turn off the heat to stop cooking but keep on stove to retain warmth of the mixture while you place one slice of *white* unbleached bread on each plate. Spoon the liver and juices over each bread slice, serving immediately. This is a last-minute preparation dish and should be made just before the guests are served. The bread soaks up the juices, which adds to the success of the dish.

Raw Vegetable Plate

Make this the day before and refrigerate in plastic bags to keep cold and crisp before arranging attractively for serving. Choose from carrot sticks, celery sticks, green onions, radishes, green pepper rings, olives, both green and ripe. Make it colorful and crisp. No dips.

44   Fabulous Nut Cake

This is the most unusual cake I have ever tasted and the credit goes to Beatrice Trum Hunter who has included it in her book, *The Natural Foods Cookbook*. The recipe contains no flour at all. Another show stopper.

    10 eggs, separated
    1 cup raw sugar
    ¾ pound unsalted nuts of any kind, or combined,
        ground fine. (I omit peanuts)
    1 teaspoon vanilla

Beat egg yolks with sugar until light and creamy. Add vanilla. Fold in stiffly-beaten egg whites. Then gently add ground nuts, folding in a few at a time. Turn into a well-oiled (angel food) tube pan or as second choice only, two 8-inch layer cake pans. Bake at 325°, one hour for tube pan or 40 to 45 minutes for layer cake pans.

This cake doesn't require a frosting. A drift of confectioners' sugar dusted through a strainer would do, or if you insist, spread lightly with powdered milk frosting: 2 tablespoons butter, 1/3 cup honey, 1 to 2 tablespoons cream or top milk and 1/4 cup powdered milk, plus 1 teaspoon vanilla. Cream butter and honey; add cream and vanilla, blend in powdered milk, adding more cream or powdered milk to make the desired consistency. (This frosting recipe comes from Agnes Toms' book, *Eat, Drink and Be Healthy*, a gourmet health cookbook and one of my favorites.)

Menu X

Spring Luncheon

Cold Avocado and Fresh Asparagus Soup
Hot Popovers
Fruit in Season
Minted Iced Tea

Avocado and Fresh Asparagus Soup

This winner is the brainchild of Gena Larson, who has long conducted the cooking page of *Lets LIVE* magazine.

She intended the soup to be served hot. I serve it iced cold. You may try it both ways and choose whichever method you think best. To make, use:

1 cup of broken fresh young asparagus spears cooked **47**
    lightly in only a few tablespoons of water
1 large avocado, peeled and cubed
2 cups of half-and-half
½ teaspoon *each* Spice Islands "fines herbs"
    seasoning, and dill weed
½ teaspoon sea salt
1 teaspoon dried onion flakes

Drop cooked asparagus and juice into your blender and purée.

Add avocado, cream, and seasoning and blend until smooth.

Add herbs, onion flakes and salt.

(If asparagus is old, you may have to run it through a strainer or food mill after cooking to remove "strings.")

Chill the soup overnight or for several hours and serve cold, topped with a dash of curry powder or chopped chives. A bowl is practically a meal in itself.

Popovers

This recipe comes from Agnes Toms' cookbook, *Eat, Drink and Be Healthy* and are they good!

Pre-heat your oven to 450°. Oil muffin pans and pre-heat them, also, for a few minutes. Popovers have no leavening. They depend upon air beaten into the batter to make them rise. The more air, the higher the popovers. Also, baking at high heat helps the popovers to rise. After they have risen, the oven is turned lower to strengthen their walls so they will stand up by themselves. NEVER open the oven door while cooking popovers, or they will fall flat.

1 cup cold milk
1 cup unbleached white flour
2 tablespoons oil
½ teaspoon salt
3 eggs

48

Place all ingredients in a bowl or blender, beating *hard* for 5 minutes. Pour batter into hot oiled muffin pans (half filled) and bake at 475° for the first 15 minutes, then lower to 400° for 15 minutes. After that time you can peek into the oven. If they are high and brown and firm to the touch, turn off the oven. They will keep warm without side effects.

Serve with plenty of butter, passing only a few popovers at a time to keep them hot. If any are left over, they make good shells for creamed chipped beef or chicken or turkey another day. Freeze them in a plastic bag.

After this meal, most people won't care whether they have dessert or not. Serve fresh fruit, but make it light.

Menu XI

Elegant Dinner

Scalloped Chicken
Green Peas
Green Salad with Regular or
Special French Dressing
Banana Crêpes with Apricot Sauce
Cups of Black Coffee with a Twist of Lemon Peel Added

This elegant dinner is, admittedly, a time-taker to prepare, but will be well worth it when you reap your reward of the delicious results and the "oohs" and "aahs" of your guests.

It will serve twelve generously, so it's good for a crowd. Once prepared in advance it will largely take care of itself. So will the dessert. The Banana-Apricot crêpes were brought to my attention by my friend, Joanna B., who serves them to drop-ins during the Christmas season, followed by raves from all who eat them.

To prepare this feast, you'd better cancel all other commitments the day before and spend the day with enjoyment preparing both the chicken and the crêpes. Here's how:

Scalloped Chicken

- 1 5-lb. chicken (a stewing hen if possible)
- Put the *whole* chicken including giblets etc. in a kettle with two quarts of water, a carrot, an onion, and 2 teaspoons salt. Bring to a boil, reduce heat and simmer until *just* done.
- Do not overcook. Cool bird in stock, then remove meat gently from bones. Cut into bite sizes and refrigerate until next day. Leave fat on the surface of the broth. Return bones, skin and giblets with stock to the pot and boil 45 minutes longer to reduce to one quart of rich broth. Put skin and giblets with some of the stock into the blender and purée or run through a grinder and add to the broth for further richness. Retain fat.

While your chicken is cooking, make your favorite recipe for stuffing. If you don't have one, use mine, which is simple:

Follow directions on the outside of a bag of Pepperidge Farm herb-flavored stuffing (reserving a few dried crumbs for topping later), then adding chopped onion, celery stalks and tops, and parsley to the remainder. Also refrigerate until the next day when you start to pull the whole thing together, about 1½ hours before serving. Now for the last-minute custard sauce which is the secret of this dish, made just prior to cooking on serving day only.

52   Custard Gravy

Remove chicken pieces, broth, and stuffing from refrigerator. Rescue firmed fat from top of broth and save. For the custard you will need:

1 cup of chicken fat or added butter if necessary to round out amount
3 tablespoons unbleached flour
1 teaspoon salt
2 cups of milk plus broth
4 eggs

In a large saucepan, put in chicken fat and melt at low heat. Add flour and stir until smooth. Gradually add milk and broth, stirring constantly until smooth and bubbly. If it becomes too thick, add more milk. DO NOT BURN. Add salt. Set off the burner to avoid scorching. Beat the eggs lightly in a bowl, stir a little of the hot gravy into the beaten eggs and then return this mixture to the remaining. (This method prevents curdling.) Return to low heat, taste for seasoning and correct, stirring constantly, for three or four minutes. Remove from heat. It will start to set as a custard.

To Assemble Dish:

Choose your largest, most attractive casserole dish or two smaller ones. Put a layer of half the stuffing on the bottom. Spoon over it half the custard gravy, then arrange half the chicken pieces on top of the gravy. Repeat the layers. On the very top, sprinkle the reserved dry stuffing crumbs. Dot with butter or margarine. Bake in a 375° oven for 20 minutes or until piping hot all the way through.

Turn off oven but keep warm. Serve buffet-style with quickly cooked green peas in another casserole and your large salad bowl.

Now for that mouth-watering dessert.

This recipe is for 8 crêpes. If you have your own favorite recipe for the crêpes, fine. Joanna keeps them made weeks ahead, in the freezer. Separate with waxed paper for easy removal. If you do not have a crêpe recipe, here is one for you. You may make them the day before and keep refrigerated. It makes 8 crêpes.

Crêpes

½ cup unsifted unbleached flour
2 tablespoons melted butter or margarine or
   vegetable oil
1 whole egg plus 1 egg yolk
¾ cup milk

1. Beat all ingredients in a blender until smooth. Cover, and refrigerate for 30 minutes.

2. Slowly heat a 7" skillet unless you have a crêpe maker. It is hot enough when a drop of water added to the pan sizzles and rolls off. For each crêpe, brush pan with butter. Pour in about 3 tablespoons batter and rotate pan to spread the batter as thinly as possible over the bottom.

3. Cook until lightly browned, then turn over on other side to brown. Turn out onto wire rack. Stack with waxed paper between each one.

Crêpe Filling

1 12 oz. jar apricot preserves
8 small or medium size bananas
¼ cup lemon juice
Butter or margarine
2 tablespoons brown sugar

1. Melt preserves with a little water in a saucepan. Stir occasionally and heat for 10 minutes.

2. Peel bananas. Brush with lemon juice. Gently sauté and turn each banana in butter for about 5 minutes or until bananas are barely tender, not mushy.

3. Spread one side of one crêpe with 1 tablespoon of the apricot sauce. Add one banana, and fold crêpe around it. (Secure with toothpick if necessary.) Repeat with remaining crêpes and bananas.

54

4. Combine butter and brown sugar in a covered chafing dish (if you don't have one, an electric frying pan turned to lowest heat will do). Add stuffed crêpes. Top with remaining apricot sauce, cover and cook 5 minutes longer. Serve one crêpe to each guest with some of the apricot sauce spooned over the crêpe. Crêpes can be stuffed and placed in chafing dish ahead of dinner time and turned on to warm during the first course.

Menu XII

Easy Dinner

Swinger (or Deluxe Hamburger)
or Deviled Hamburger (no buns)
Baked Potato
Green Salad
Fruit Frappé

Swinger Hamburgers

The Swinger hamburger came from the famous Aware Inn gourmet health restaurant in Los Angeles. It is a full meal in itself. Youngsters, teenagers and adults love it. I can only give you ingredients, not amounts. Choose enough to suit the number you wish to serve.

Hamburger or chopped meat
Chopped onion, red preferably, for appearance
Fresh tomato, chopped
Shredded cheddar cheese
Wheat germ
Egg, beaten
Sea salt, plus pinch of oregano
Few drops of Worcestershire

Combine all and make into patties or mounds. You can fry the patties, but the Aware Inn made them in mounds, covered them individually with an inverted stainless steel bowl and steamed them on a frying pan until cooked through.

Or try:

Deviled Hamburgers

> 1 lb. hamburger
> 2 tablespoons chili sauce
> 3 teaspoons prepared mustard
> 1 teaspoon horseradish
> 1 small clove of garlic minced or mashed
> 1 teaspoon Worcestershire sauce
> 2 teaspoons grated onion
> 1 teaspoon salt. Pepper if desired.
> Broil or pan fry.

Fruit Frappé is one of my most cherished recipes. I was introduced to it in a unique coffee house where it was served in a glass bowl with a foot (like a huge champagne glass). The frappé was made on the spot from fresh fruit and the customer sipped it through a straw. It was dramatic to see and delicious to taste. Since the coffee house owners have moved away, these fruit frappés are no longer available there. You will have to experiment with them and find something dramatic and unusual to serve them in. Perhaps a giant mug, or an extra tall glass; I'll leave it up to you.

58   To get the recipe I watched them make it, and here is my version.

Fruit Frappe

In a blender, put one whole fruit: a peeled orange, cut into sections, or a lemon, or peach, or banana, or some fresh pineapple, or berries of any kind, or any desired combination. (Believe it or not the orange was the most popular.)

Add: ½ cup of milk or yogurt
½ cup crushed ice
1 teaspoon vanilla — no matter what fruit is used
— this *makes* it!
Honey to taste (2 teaspoons for orange, more for
lemon, etc.)

Blend furiously until smooth and frothy. Serve, with a straw, in the most dramatic glass you can find.

Menu XIII

"Airport" Dinner

Saffron Chicken-and-Rice
Green Salad and Croutons
Quick Cooked Green Vegetable in Season
Fresh Pineapple Slices with Lace Cookies

This is another help-yourself meal for guests or family.
Saffron Chicken is one of those recipes I cut out of a paper. It has been worth its weight in gold. I especially fall back upon this dish when I have to meet a plane and pick up a traveller who arrives ravenous. The "Airport" chicken cooks untended and is ready when we return home. The dessert was made earlier and I throw the salad together while the vegetable is cooking. Dinner is ready by the time the hungry, tired person has taken off a coat and washed hands.

61

Saffron Chicken

    1 chicken fryer, cut up
    Garlic salt
    ¼ teaspoon Spanish saffron. (It is expensive but goes a
        long way. It takes more than 100,000 hand picked

blooms of autumn-flowering crocus from Spain to make a pound of the dried orange stigmas which give an interesting flavor and beautiful color to the rice.)

¾ cups of brown rice
2½ cups salted water
9 tablespoons raisins
¼ cup (1 package) of almond bits or slices

Sprinkle each piece of chicken liberally with garlic salt. Place on a shallow broiling pan and broil at highest heat until crispy, and excess fat has run off. Remove chicken from the pan and discard fat.

Start rice boiling in the salted water-plus-saffron in a covered pan until it begins to soften and most of the water has been absorbed. Add raisins and nuts. Place rice, nuts and raisins plus liquid in the bottom of a roasting pan. Lay chicken pieces on top and cover. Put in a preheated 325° oven, and turn heat down immediately to 225°. Bake for two hours, more or less (more is not fatal), or until all water has been absorbed by the rice and the chicken is tender. You have to eat this unusual dish to appreciate it. I haven't found anyone yet who didn't like it.

For dessert, your fresh pineapple has already been prepared, and the slices are refrigerated. I will give you two recipes for lace cookies, also to be prepared in advance. One recipe is easy, the other is more difficult. Use the one you prefer, depending upon the time you have for preparation. I opt for the more difficult, which is also the more delicious version. Here it is:

Almond Lace Wafers

¾ cup finely sliced unblanched almonds (Can be hand-grated or ground in the blender)
¼ cup butter or margarine
¼ cup raw sugar
1 tablespoon flour
2 tablespoons half-and-half
1 teaspoon vanilla

Combine all ingredients. Cook in a small heavy pan over low heat until the butter melts, stirring constantly. Add vanilla after removing from heat. Drop by heaping teaspoonful on a flour-dusted cookie sheet, making only a few cookies at a time and spacing them about 3 inches apart. Bake at 350° about 9 minutes or until light brown and still bubbling in the center. Let cool only until the edge is firm enough to lift off with a thin spatula. Lay on individual layers of waxed paper or another wide cookie sheet or tray. A fresh cookie sheet should be used for each baking to prevent the cookies from sticking. Yield: about 3 dozen wafers. Store unused wafers in an airtight dry container.

Easy Lace Cookies

    3 cups brown sugar
    3 cups oatmeal
    ¾ cup melted butter or margarine
    1 teaspoon vanilla
    2 unbeaten eggs

Mix and bake at 350° on seasoned pans.

Menu XIV

Fish Dinner
Baked Filet of Sole
Quick Creamed Potatoes
Green Peas
Green Salad with Croutons
Spiced Granola Apple Crisp

Baked Filet of Sole

Mike and Mary Spencer, authors of that charmer, *The* **65** *Ultimate Soup Cook Book* (Mike is an ex-editor of *Lets LIVE* magazine) found this recipe for sole filet. It is incredibly easy and good. Butter the bottom of a flat pyrex oblong baking dish. Lay the filets flat on the buttered dish. Spread tops of filets with savory mayonnaise (I use Best Foods — known in the East as Hellmann's) and top that with a sprinkle of Pepperidge Farm herb-flavored stuffing bread crumbs. Dot with butter and bake at 325° until fish is white and tender. About 25 minutes, but don't overcook until dry or tough. Serve with lemon wedges.

Quick Creamed Potatoes

This is another recipe one of my daughters discovered in a New York City newspaper and I laugh every time I make it. The reason: I served it once while I was living on the East coast and a vice-president of the United States and his wife were present. The wife huddled with the other women guests trying to figure out what the dish was — spaghetti or what? No one guessed it until they asked me. All of them asked for the recipe.

Peel and grate 5 medium raw potatoes into a saucepan. Cover with whole milk or half-and-half. Add 2 tablespoons butter, one grated onion, salt and pepper. Simmer gently, stirring occasionally until potatoes are tender and milk is absorbed, leaving a creamy consistency. Sprinkle with chopped parsley. If the potatoes are finely grated, this recipe will take about 10 minutes. Be careful not to Scorch! Serves 6. (Leftovers can be combined with egg and made into potato pancakes the next day.)

The green peas can be fresh or frozen.

By now you have discovered that I serve green salad with every meal. (See Menu I)

Spiced Granola Apple Crisp

Another newspaper finding! Said the paper, "Once tried will often be eaten." You'd better believe it. It's true.

66 Spiced Granola (can also be used as a breakfast cereal)

    4 cups old-fashioned oats
    1 can (4 oz.) shredded coconut
    ½ cup sesame seed
    ½ cup toasted wheat germ
    1½ teaspoons ground cinnamon
    1 teaspoon ground nutmeg
    ½ cup honey
    ½ cup oil
    1 cup dark raisins

Combine dry ingredients except raisins in a large bowl. Add honey and oil. Mix well. Pour onto a large flat cookie sheet, spread contents out, and bake at 350° until golden, about 15 minutes, stirring occasionally. Remove from oven, cool, crumble and add raisins. Keeps best refrigerated.

If you are in a tearing hurry, or have other granola already on hand, you can add the spices to it, put all in a plastic bag, close and shake vigorously. Not quite as good, but will pass.

Spiced Granola Apple Crisp

6 cups of peeled apple slices. (Apples should be tart and firm, not mushy when cooked. Ask your grocer before buying.)
½ cup raw or brown sugar
2 tablespoons flour
1 teaspoon apple pie spice or the equivalent of cinnamon and nutmeg. (I can't find the apple pie spice in the stores.)
2 teaspoons lemon juice
¼ teaspoon salt
2 teaspoons butter or margarine, divided
1 cup spiced granola, divided

To assemble:

In a large bowl combine apples, sugar, flour, lemon juice, spice and salt. In a buttered 1½ quart casserole, place one half of this mixture. Dot with 1 tablespoon butter. Repeat the layer. Cover and bake at 375° until apples are tender (about 45 minutes). Serves 8. It is best warm, but acceptable the next day cold. Serve with cream or ice cream if you wish.

Menu XV

Unusual Dinner
Lemon Chicken
Potato Pancakes
Vegetable in Season (Optional)
Green Salad
Lemon Squares (cookies)

Lemon Chicken

69

Cut chicken in individual pieces
Combine 2/3 cup lemon juice with 1/3 cup water and marinate chicken in it for at least two hours, turning as needed.

Remove chicken and drop each piece in a bag with lightly salted unbleached flour. Shake to coat and remove. Place all pieces in a single layer on a flat baking pan. Top each piece with a pat of butter, a slice of lemon and sprinkle brown sugar on top of lemon. Bake at 325° until brown, approximately one hour.

Potato Pancakes

Grate 4 large potatoes and 1 small onion.
Add: ½ cup milk
     1 beaten egg
     2 tablespoons flour
     1 teaspoon salt

Mix and drop by spoonful on hot griddle, browning on both sides.

Lemon Squares

These cookies are yummy. If you have any left, serve them to guests for afternoon tea. They freeze well; but warm them after thawing them.

In an 8″ x 8″ pyrex flat baking dish, spread a graham cracker crumb crust. Then add:

Filling:

2 eggs
1 scant cup brown sugar
¾ cup regular granola (not spiced)
½ cup chopped walnuts
1 teaspoon vanilla
2 tablespoons flour
⅛ teaspoon baking powder

Mix well, add to top of crumb crust and bake at 350° until brown.

Icing

½ cup powdered sugar or ¼ cup honey
1½ tablespoon lemon juice
1 teaspoon grated lemon peel

Combine ingredients and drizzle over the hot baked batter immediately *after* removing from oven. Let cool slightly and cut into squares.

Menu XVI

Simple Sunday Night Supper
Welsh Rarebit
Raw Finger Food: carrot sticks, scallions
cauliflower rosettes, radishes, green pepper strips,
celery, olives. Pickles if desired.
Hot Gingerbread with Butter or Ice Cream

This Welsh Rarebit recipe has been in our family for a long time. We have eaten many other recipes, but prefer this one. It can be made in an electric fry pan at the table.

Welsh Rarebit

1 egg per person
Less than ½ cup milk per egg
Approximately ½ cup sharp cheddar cheese or less
    per person
½ teaspoon Worcestershire sauce
¼ teaspoon mustard powder
Salt
A little butter and a little flour

In fry pan melt cheese together with butter and a shake of flour. Add beaten yolks mixed with milk and stir until smooth. Add Worcestershire sauce and mustard powder.

(Or all can be put in blender except egg whites before putting in fry pan.)

Just before serving, add beaten egg whites, and fold in lightly.

Serve on thin crisp melta toast or crackers.

Sprinkle with paprika.

Gingerbread

Put 2 heaping tablespoons brown sugar in a cup and fill with Brer Rabbit Yellow Label Molasses or ½ honey and ½ blackstrap molasses.

Wet Ingredients

Mix: ½ cup oil
½ cup milk
1 beaten egg
molasses mixture

Add to: Dry Ingredients

2 scant cups unbleached flour
1 heaping teaspoon baking powder
1 level teaspoon soda
½ teaspoon ginger

Combine mixtures and stir until smooth. Do not beat. Bake in flat greased pan at 325-350° until firm. Be careful not to burn.

Or, if you don't mind cheating, instead of starting from scratch, use Dromedary Gingerbread Mix. I have used it for years. It is made from a recipe supposedly supplied by Martha Washington, wife of George Washington. It is available in most grocery stores. It is the only mix I use.

Menu XVII

French Dinner
French Sweetbreads
Green Salad
French Peas
Brown Rice
Dry White Wine
Cheese Cake

French Sweetbreads (Can also be made with diced cooked white meat of chicken but it's not as delicate or good.)

It took me three solid years to get this recipe. I first ate it at a French restaurant and immediately requested the recipe. I was told by the owner that the only way I could get it was to write to a certain gourmet magazine, asking them to publish it. I did. No recipe. I returned to the restaurant and began again. Same routine. This kept up for three years. Finally, in desperation, I appealed to the owner's wife (now a friend since I had been there so often) who gave me the recipe for my birthday. Wouldn't you know it? The next week the recipe was published in that gourmet magazine!

Cook the brown rice ahead of time and keep it warm.

The French peas are the tiny canned or frozen variety, heated with a bit of sugar, chopped scallion tops (later removed) and seasoned with butter. I took Adelle Davis to this restaurant once (now too expensive to take anyone) and though the peas came with the meal, she said she didn't want any. But after she tasted mine, she reneged and asked for a large dish.

French Sweetbreads

Cook ½ pound of sweetbreads per person in cold, salted water until barely tender. Save juice to add to rice cooking water. Cool. Cut into bite sizes.

Empty one 8 oz. size carton of *real* whipping cream (natural, NOT artificial) into a flat sauce pan. (One 8 oz. container of cream serves two people.)

Slice approximately six medium-sized mushrooms per person and add with cubed sweetbreads to the heavy cream. Add 1 generous tablespoon of Malmsey Rozès Madeira wine for *each* person. NO SUBSTITUTE WILL WORK. This is the secret of this dish. Let the mixture bubble, uncovered, until thick.

This will take about one-half hour.

Taste and add perhaps one shake (no more) of salt if necessary. This dish has a delicate flavor and is the kind of creation that should cause you to scream if anyone at the table adds salt before tasting.

Serve with rice and the most expensive dry white French wine you can afford. This dish is not for a crowd. Reserve it to serve "a deux" with your husband, wife, lover, or best friend. Only gourmets will appreciate it.

Cheese Cake

This is my recipe, not French, and though originally borrowed from a dear friend, Midge, is better than any cheese cake I have ever tasted and I have tasted many. It *must* ripen in the pan in the refrigerator for at least four to five days before eating. So prepare it in advance, accordingly.

Beat with an electric beater for 20 minutes until smooth:

½ lb. Philadelphia cream cheese
½ lb. creamed cottage cheese
½ lb. Farmer's cheese or regular small curd cottage cheese
¾ cup raw sugar (honey will not work)
3 eggs
1 teaspoon vanilla

Make a graham cracker crumb crust and put on the bottom of a spring form pan. Pour batter on top and bake for 20 minutes at 350°.

While it is baking, stir into a large container 2 cups yogurt or sour cream, 2 tablespoons raw sugar, and 1 scant teaspoon vanilla.

Remove cake from oven. Spread second mixture over the top and return the cake to the oven. Bake 5 minutes longer at 450°.

When cool, cover with a plate or foil, and refrigerate for four to five days. It will then be smooth, creamy and velvety.

Menu XVIII

Home-made Vegetable Soup

I have one friend, Charlotte, who would never forgive me if I did not include my recipe for home-made vegetable soup. She is a nutrition consultant and has told others far and wide that it is the best soup she has ever tasted. Unfortunately, this is a recipe which includes this-and-that, so I can only give you an approximate idea of what goes into it, plus lots of love, since I love to make it.

I keep vegetable odds and ends in a plastic bag in my refrigerator or freezer. These may include asparagus stems, leftover pieces of onion and scallion tops, celery and leaves, green pepper, tomato, carrot, parsley and so on.

When cold weather is imminent I start the brew in a crockpot, beginning with anything in the meat department which will provide a good rich broth. It may be soup bones and meat, neck bones — anything cheap and tough which will provide flavor. I then add the pieces of vegetable odds and ends, plus extra onion, a clove of garlic, cover it all with water and add salt, and perhaps add a pinch of oregano. *I cook it on low all night long!*

The next day I fish out the odds and ends and throw them in the compost. If the brew needs more flavor I add an undiluted can of Campbell's Consommé. After that I cut up fresh vegetables, including more onion, celery, carrots, tomatoes fresh or canned, and let simmer in the broth for several hours more on low, or if necessary, turn it to high to cook quickly, but in any case *under*-cook the fresh vegetables, which I like bright-colored and on the crisp side. I ladle out the soup into large earthenware cups, serve with a spoon at first, leaving the dregs to be drunk from the cup. Simple but satisfying.

If any is left, it freezes well.

Menu XIX

Thanksgiving Dinner or a Buffet

The crux of Thanksgiving, of course, is the turkey. But since it is popular and now less expensive than ham or roast beef, it also can serve as an excellent buffet entrée any time of the year. For this reason I want to share with you the method of cooking a turkey I learned from Adelle Davis, which is not only easy, but *always* moist. I cannot abide a dry turkey and when I see the various methods people use to prevent dryness, ranging from plastic bags to buttered muslin, even foil, and still have a turkey dryer than I like, I feel sorry for them and for all that unecessary effort. So whether you cook it stuffed, for Thanksgiving, or un-stuffed for a buffet, the recipe is the same:

Place the turkey, stuffed or unstuffed, on a low rack in a *covered* roaster. Put a small amount of water in the bottom, under the rack, making certain the water does not touch the turkey. Cover and simmer gently on the top of the stove. Remember, the water should quiver, only. When the drumstick moves easily, and the meat looks white, it is done. I cannot tell you how long, exactly, because it depends on the size and age of your turkey. It takes approximately 1½ to 2 hours. Do not allow steam to escape from the pan during cooking.

When it is done, remove from roaster and transfer to a flat pan. Rub the turkey with a stick of butter or margarine and place in a 325° oven until browned to perfection. This may take another hour.

The only trouble with this technique is that all the juices do not escape from the turkey into the pan or gravy, if any.

When it is carved, juice may then spurt out. You may have to fortify the gravy — if you make it — with broth from cooking the giblets separately, and other addenda. But the turkey, I guarantee, will never be dry.

The first time I used this method was on Thanksgiving. I recklessly put it on the stove and went to church. I didn't have a peaceful minute while there, but when I returned in about 1½ hours, it was perfect. I then oven-browned it and have used no other method since.

On Thanksgiving, I often serve in the livingroom, before the guests come to the table, mugs of hot juice, made by combining equal parts of orange juice and tomato juice which have simmered with a cinnamon stick and a couple of cloves or so for an hour or more. Children don't like it, but adults do.

Whether for Thanksgiving or buffet, I always serve the following Salad Fruit Mold. One friend was invited to her mother-in-law's home for Thanksgiving, and took this salad mold with her. The next year, she was invited again. "But," said the mother-in-law, "don't come without that wonderful salad mold." Here it is:

Fruit Mold

    1 can of black cherries, pitted, or 1 container frozen
       black cherries, pitted
    1 lb. raw cranberries, ground with 2 oranges and a
       little grated peel
    2 cups of any juice: cranberry, orange and black
       cherry juice you can rescue, plus enough water to
       produce two cups total of liquid

Heat, according to directions and mix with 1 box (3 oz.) Black Cherry Jello and 1 box (3 ox.) Raspberry Jello.

Add fruit and taste. If not sweet enough for you, add up to ¼ cup raw sugar. Then add ½ to 1 cup whole pecans, or pieces.

Pour in mold pan and refrigerate until firm, or pour into individual custard cups and unmold when ready to serve.

The rest of the Thanksgiving menu is up to you.

Choose what you like.

Menu XX

Grand Finale

When you really want to make a splash, this is IT. Set your table and buffet with the most colorful dishes and glassware you have. Use Oriental ware if you have it, otherwise combine ingenuity, color and unexpected table arrangements for dramatic effect. If you have a special collection, now is the time to use it. Anything goes, just so it is different and eye-catching.

This menu was photographed in color, quite a few years ago in *House Beautiful,* and the menu, based on curried turkey with condiments, is the brainchild of Virginia Stanton, former party editor of *House Beautiful.* The recipe, minus those photographs (but there are other gorgeous ones) also appears in the book by Virginia Stanton, the *House Beautiful Guide to Successful Entertaining.* If you say you don't like curry, don't skip this until you have read it all. People who don't like curry, like this dish; even men!

You can use leftover Thanksgiving turkey, 8 cups of white meat and a little dark meat, or buy individual turkey parts, cook them and save the well-seasoned broth. When Virginia Stanton's children were at home, they always urged her to get the biggest Thanksgiving turkey possible so there would be enough left over for this extravaganza, which they liked better than in the original role as Thanksgiving turkey.

Here is the recipe for the sauce, plus the assortment of condiments to be served with the dish. (The condiments really help provide the drama.)

First, make a large casserole of brown rice and put aside to keep hot.

While the rice is cooking, arrange the condiments, either on a lazy susan, or a pretty tray of attractive small dishes, with a separate dish and spoon for each. Assemble the following condiments, one type in each dish:

- Chopped mixed nuts
- Coconut, fresh shredded, canned, or toasted (available in cans)
- Cubed banana, sprinkled with lemon juice to avoid turning brown (toasted banana chips are another possibility)
- Major Grey or other chutney — a *must*
- Chopped green onions (scallions) with leaves for color

Other additions are welcome such as raisins, etc.

Search the Oriental section of your grocery store for other ideas.

Curry Sauce for Turkey

90   Cut 8 heaping cups of turkey meat, mostly white, into large bite size and put aside while you make the sauce:

½ pound butter or margarine
1 medium onion cut up fine
2 *level* tablespoons curry powder
2 cups of well-seasoned turkey broth
2½ cups of milk
½ cup unbleached white flour
1 Ripe banana
1 apple, cored, peeled and cut into slices
Salt to taste

In your largest frying pan, melt the butter, sauté the onion lightly and blend in the curry powder with a wooden spoon. In the blender, put some of the soup stock, flour, banana and apple slices, and purée. Add remainder of liquid to pan and also pour puréed mixture slowly into frying pan, stirring constantly to keep sauce bubbly. Taste for salt and add accordingly. Add the turkey at the last minute only, allowing it to heat, but lower heat of burner and do not stir or meat will become stringy. Transfer all to a large casserole and keep hot.

The order of exercises: each guest is to help himself to rice and curry, then the condiments. The curry newcomer usually begins by adding a dab of each condiment very cautiously on his plate beside the rice-curry servings, but, like sophisticated curry fans, soon returns for a refill, dumping them all helter-skelter over the whole turkey-rice mixture.

As Virginia Stanton says, "They eat up and say, 'Terrific.'"

This menu needs little else except something tart and crunchy, such as a large crisp green salad in a bowl which should be served flanked by individual bowls or salad plates so as not to overload the already crowded plate of the rice-turkey and condiments.

A fresh fruit cup, followed by coffee, rounds out the menu. Your guests will remember it for weeks.

Voila!

Miscellaneous After-Thoughts

Stuffed Mushrooms: *an h'ors d'oeuvre*

This recipe was served at a cocktail party in New York City. One of the guests, a friend of mine, was so excited over it, she phoned her mother long distance in a Western state and gave her the recipe over the phone! Later she gave it to me. Although more and more people are eating raw mushrooms, I would suggest, when you serve them that you not call attention to the fact the mushrooms are raw. Usually guests don't notice it when they see them on the serving plate. Afterward there are never any left because they are so delicious. Guests who take one gingerly usually smack their lips and ask for more.

The recipe

16 even size mushrooms, preferably white. Stem and save stems for later cooking purposes

Mix ¼ lb. Philadelphia cream cheese, ½ cup sour cream, 1 tablespoon Worcestershire sauce till smooth

Add 1 2 oz. can of chopped pimientos (or a small bottle of pimiento-stuffed green olives chopped as a substitute) and 1 2-oz. can of anchovies, drained and cut into small pieces with scissors. I often scrape in a little raw onion juice, but this is optional.

Let this mixture ripen a few hours in the refrigerator. Just before serving time, fill mushroom caps with the mixture and add a shake of paprika on the top of each. Arrange on a serving plate.

A Superior Birthday Cake

Make an angel food cake from your favorite mix, available in stores. After it has cooled, with a sharp knife, slice the top off carefully, about ½ inch thick. Set aside. With a sharp-pointed knife, cut close (½") to the inside wall of the cake to loosen it, then insert the knife point about ½ inch from the bottom, sliding and cutting from one entrance point if possible, all across the lower part of the cake, and lift out the interior. This leaves a ½ inch cake shell.

Beat one small container of whipping cream stiff, add a few drops of vanilla and fold in a container of juice-free whole fresh or frozen raspberries. Fill the cake cavity with this mixture. Return the top of the cake as a cover.

Whip a second container of whipping cream, adding a heaping teaspoon of sugar and ½ teaspoon vanilla. Use this as icing. Spread it over the entire cake. Refrigerate, until ready to serve. (Should be made the same day it is used.) When you cut this cake and lay each piece on its side; it is pretty as well as luscious. Ice cream is not needed.

94

Baked Corn on the Cob

In fresh corn season I cook my corn in two ways:

1. Shuck ears of corn. Place in a large pot with a *small* amount of water. Do *not* cover the corn with water. Cover the pot, bring small amount of water to boil and steam for a few minutes only — until corn is fork-tender. This retains much of the flavor so often lost by covering it with water.

2. Better yet, leave the ears in their shucks. If you are barbecuing outdoors, lay the ears-in-shucks on the coals,

turning from time to time. Or, still easier, put ears still in shucks in a 350° oven and bake until the green shucks turn the color of straw. Remove, shuck immediately with hot mitts, then butter. All flavor is retained this way.

The feedback on this corn is so great that I now do not cook it any other way.

Butter Stretcher

For those who would like to make a spread which is more healthful than margarine and cheaper than butter, here is a treasured formula:

1 lb. butter
1 cup natural vegetable oil (soy, safflower or blend — from health store)
2-4 tablespoons lecithin (from health stores)

It may be in granule, powder or liquid form. I use liquid. All lecithin is made from soy beans.

Dissolve the lecithin in the oil in a blender. Let butter soften at room temperature and add the liquid oil — lecithin mixture. Beat all until smooth with an electric beater. (If the liquid lecithin clings to the inside of the spoon or blender wipe off with a dry paper towel before washing.

Store entire mixture in covered containers in a refrigerator. It will spread easily on removal from the refrigerator. If you like more salt, add a bit of sea salt before mixing.

This formula was contributed by nutritionists from The Resort of The Mountains (near Tacoma, Washington). They state, according to recent findings, that the addition of the oil supplies essential fatty acids; the lecithin dissolves cholesterol; and the combination helps to build up insulation around the nerves.

This spread is good for baked potatoes, vegetables, toast and breads. The variations are endless: for garlic

95

butter, add crushed or minced garlic. For herb butter, add a *small* amount of Fines Herbs (Spice Islands).

For gifts, give it plain in a small attractive plastic container and let the recipient do his/her thing with it.

How To Eat Right Day-In, Day-Out: A Way of Life

As you now know, in order to keep your body in optimum condition, you need to use the right fuel regularly, although I hope that the recipes which precede this section have proved to be a pleasant interlude. But let the interlude be the exception, not the rule. Why?

These foods are not actually junk foods, which merely taste good but fill you up without anything for you. Still, there are too many no-nos among these recipes to assure good health if taken on a regular basis. It really is true that *you are what you eat.* If you eat wholesome, natural, nutritious foods, you will be supplying your body with repair materials which it can use to keep you in good repair. I have seen it work again and again for all types of people, so it is not a coincidence that there is a correlation between what you eat, day-in, day-out, and health.

99

How Can You Protect Yourself?

Read your labels before buying! If you can't pronounce the name of a chemical on the label, don't eat it! (This does not apply to vitamins and minerals with long names.)

What Can You Eat?

You can eat whole, natural foods. These include:

Natural brown rice

Whole grain cereals and flours

Natural, unheated, unfiltered honey (in small amounts. No sweetening should be over-used.) Avoid honey labelled "Pure deluxe" meaning that nutrients have usually been removed.

Fresh, raw foods. These contain enzymes which keep you feeling and looking better. All TV and Movie Stars know this secret.

Wheat germ

Brewer's or nutritional yeast (a powerhouse of B vitamins, many minerals and protein factors). Do not eat raw baker's yeast.

Sunflower seeds (hulled), very nutritious for snacking and cooking.

Blackstrap molasses (for flavoring and cooking). Rinse mouth if taking straight since it sticks to teeth.

Lecithin

Yogurt and other cultured milks

Natural vegetable oils

Sprouted seeds (buy or make your own)

These whole foods contain repair materials, vitamins, minerals and other nutrients. Lack of space prevents me **100** from telling you what is in each one, but you will find the information in my other books, especially in *Know Your Nutrition*.

These foods are not necessarily wonder foods. They are merely richer in nutrients, so you can eat less, gain less, and save more money from not buying so many foods.

One of the best ways to switch from junk foods to good foods has been explained in *A Mini-Guide to Living Foods* published by the Price Pottenger Nutrition Foundation, 5622 Dartford Way, San Diego, California 92120. This organization is actually helping people to rebuild good health. The following information is adapted from their publication, which contains excellent recipes for healthful eating.

"Instead Of's"

— Instead of refined sugars on cereals, tart fruits or in desserts . . .
> Try raw honey, maple syrup, molasses, sorghum, dried fruits, whole raw fruit

— Instead of soda pop or other sweetened beverages . . .
> Try pure water, herb teas, fruit juices, homemade root beer and ginger ale, carob drinks and others

— Instead of candies . . .
> Try dried or fresh fruits, carob fudge, nuts, and sunflower seeds

— Instead of commercial ice creams and sherbets, pop-sickles . . .
> Try frozen bananas dipped in carob, buttermilk ice cream and homemade ice creams, sherbets, and pop-sickles

— Instead of jellies and jams . . .
> Try raw fruit jams, or homemade jams and marmalades made with honey

— Instead of pastries and pies, cookies, and cakes . . .

101

> Try Bavarian creams, natural cream puffs, carob-covered eclairs and many others.* Also cookies made from carob, fruits, seeds, nuts, raw brownies.*

*Recipes provided in *Mini Guide*

In addition to these excellent suggestions and recipes in the Price Pottenger Nutrition Foundation *Mini Guide,* you will find some other excellent cookbooks in health stores with further healthful, satisfying suggestions by Adelle Davis, Beatrice Trum Hunter, Agnes Toms and others.

Many readers ask me what I eat as well as what vitamin/mineral supplements I take. To date I have refused to answer because everyone is as different from everyone else as his fingerprints. The old saying "What is one man's meat is another man's poison" can actually be true. This applies even to people in the same family.

However, I will give you my general eating pattern though I still refuse to state my supplements, for the reasons given above.

To begin with I eat very little since I work many hours a day in a sedentary job of writing. If food is of high quality you need less. Next, I am NOT a vegetarian. I have learned too much about how the body needs protein of some kind for survival. You will find this information in my books, *Secrets of Health and Beauty* and *The Best of Linda Clark*. If you have other questions why I eat what I do, see my *Know Your Nutrition*. (These books are in paperback at health stores.)

My *Breakfast:* Fruit juice — with added lecithin
Two fresh, fertile eggs, *daily*
One piece whole grain toast with butter
One glass of raw, whole, certified milk
    plus supplements

My *Lunch:* Except for brewer's yeast this changes daily. Here is one example:
1 heaping tablespoon of brewer's yeast in water (always)
1 handful of sunflower seeds
1 raw apple or other raw fruit
    plus supplements

My *Dinner:* Protein of some kind: meat, fish, or fowl
Raw green salad
Perhaps a glass of dry red wine,
    no more than 3 oz.

Surprise Ending

Have you ever stopped to think how many meals you eat annually? Three times 365, or 1095, plus mid-meal snacks. This is why I say that if you eat even 1050 meals per year which constitute good nutrition, your health will reflect it, allowing you to have fun eating what you like especially, even though it is non-nutritional, for 45 meals per year. Of course, this may not mean you can eat *anything.* Diabetics cannot eat sugar at all, nor should those with allergies take a chance, either. For this reason, it would be greatly appreciated if, when you invite guests to your house for one of these 45 meals, you ask ahead of time if they are diabetic or allergic, and then choose or rearrange a menu accordingly.

In this day and age, more and more people are having trouble eating away from home. Restaurant food is not always carefully chosen or handled. Additives, sugar, poisons such as the heavy metals, lead, mercury and cadmium, are hidden in food, and fish from contaminated water, plus re-heated frozen dinners from unknown courses are often served. Many are complaining that they are not able to "eat out" any more because they become violently ill. I have experienced this myself and am sympathetic. Whereas I once had a long list of delightful restaurants I enjoyed, either the prices have become prohibitive or the food has stood in aluminum containers over a steam table for hours, or ingredients like those mentioned above are used. My acceptable list has dwindled to a limited number of restaurants where I *know* the food is prepared from scratch, from safe and fresh sources, and is cooked either to order or shortly before hand.

What Foods are No-Nos?

Sugar:

White sugar is completely refined, containing no vitamins or minerals of any kind. It steals B vitamins from your body, can cause cavities, heart disease, overweight, nervousness and the "new" disease, Hypoglycemia. Using sugar by the pinch, for flavoring, is one thing; by the cupful makes it a no-no *food.*

White flour:

White flour also is refined, containing no vitamins or minerals or other nutrients. If any vitamins/minerals have been added, forget it. They are synthetic, are but a drop in the bucket compared to the many natural ones removed, thus producing an incomplete food. If white flour has been bleached, run for your life! It has been found to give dogs fits, why not you? Unbleached flour is safe to eat, though not particularly nutritious.

Refined and Processed Foods

Have also been denuded of nutrients. These so-called "convenience foods" like TV dinners, etc., have had nutrients removed, and worse, additives and chemicals such as preservatives, artificial colors and flavors have been included to prolong shelf life at the grocers. Even insects cannot survive on such foods. Many tests show that these additives can cause cancer. More recent reports show that such additives are also a cause of hyperactivity in children; and headaches, fatigue and other vague ailments in adults.

Too many cases of illness or unintentional food poisonings are turning people back to their friends' or their own homes for safe eating. This may be a good thing. Our nation was fast becoming a nation of shortcut foods or TV dinner consumers. Cooking from scratch takes time but better health is the result, particularly in these times when so many people are already ailing.

But there is something more which influences the food you eat. A medical doctor in the United States once told me that his parents, who were missionaries in India, had perfect health despite the non-nutritional fare they were given in India. The doctor said, "Do you know why I think they had good health in spite of their poor food? It is because they blessed their meals before they ate them!"

We know that light, sound and color have vibrations. So does thought. If good vibrations are beamed at food, a very different product can emerge than if the same food were contaminated with bad vibes. For example, a couple whom I know well, was eating in a New York City restaurant. The wife is a well-known clairvoyant. They each ordered different foods after which the husband became violently ill, although his wife did not. Afterward, the husband asked his wife for an explanation of his illness. She said that she "saw" the chef in a violent rage when he had prepared her husband's meal. Hers had apparently been prepared earlier and therefore was uncontaminated by his angry vibes.

Plants which are blessed or handled with love, thrive. Why not food cooked with love?

I have eaten food prepared in the home of a person who loves to cook, and I thrived on that food. I have eaten similar food prepared by those who hated every minute they spent in the kitchen and the after-effects were con-

firmed by my stomach. People who don't like to cook should turn it over to someone who does, or change their attitude.

Food is a source of energy. So is love. Natural, nutritious food has more energy and better vibes than synthetic or ersatz food. That is why it is so important to eat such food. It does more for you. Add the good vibes of love and you raise the energy still higher of whatever, or whomever, you apply it to. This improves the taste as well as raising the energy of the dish you are preparing. So why not spike it with love, too? It is not hard to do. Love the food. Love your friends, guests or your family. Love cooking for them. *How* you serve is as important as *what* you serve.

But when you do this, don't be surprised when people say, "I love your cooking," or "I love to eat at your house." What they really mean is that they feel the love you have added. As someone recently stated, "Nearly everyone in the whole world is suffering from malnutrition of too little love."

This reminds me of a friend, a widow, who, years ago had very little money. I stopped at her house one afternoon and she invited me to stay for tea. She frankly admitted (but did not apologize) that her cupboard was bare, but she begged me to stay anyway and shared with me what she did have. She found one lone can of peaches on an otherwise empty kitchen shelf and added some bread and butter plus the tea. That was all she had.

But she served it with love! It tasted delicious. Since then I have been invited to many banquets and many feasts. I do not remember a single detail of any of them. But I do remember every detail of that simple tea, and I always will because it was served from the heart with love! I still feel the love whenever I think about it. So add love to the food you serve to yourself and others. It will help everyone.

And *anyone* can do it.

Index